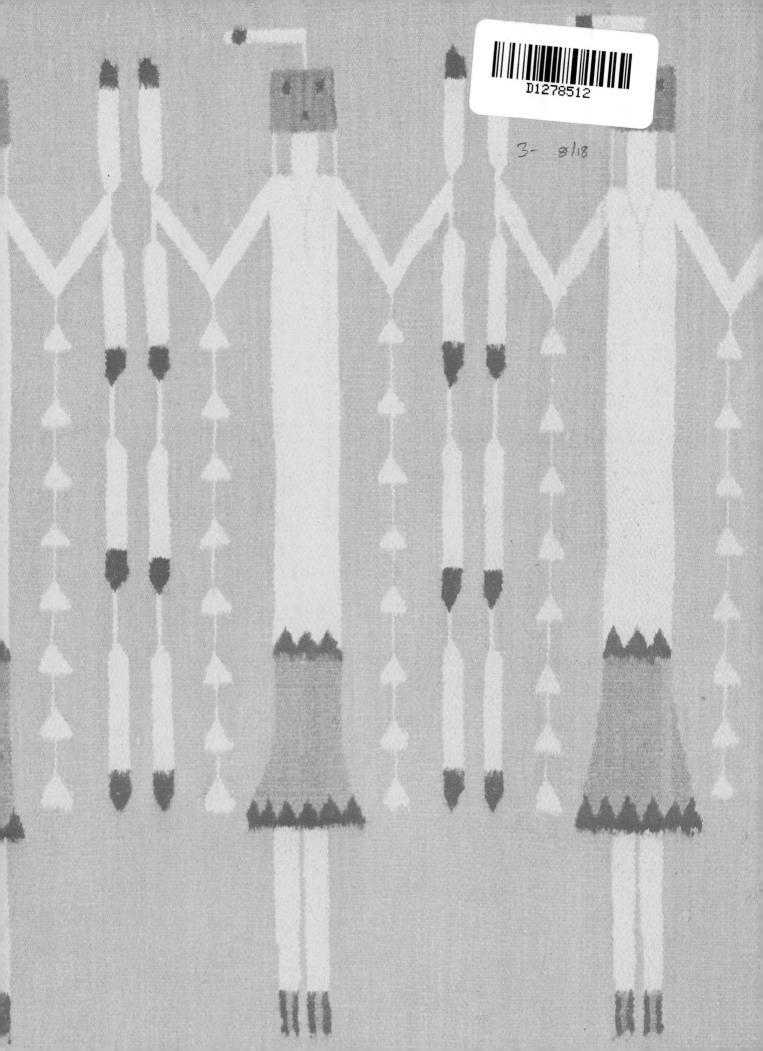

The Beautiful Southwest

A Sunset Pictorial

The Beautiful Southwest

LANE MAGAZINE & BOOK COMPANY
MENLO PARK, CALIFORNIA

Edited by
Paul C. Johnson

Coordinating Editor
Elizabeth Hogan

Design
Judith Whipple & John Flack

Cartography
John Flack

Consultants

Natural Science, *Harriett E. Weaver*
Arizona, *Merrill Windsor*
New Mexico, *Walter Briggs*
New Mexico, *Kenneth Hardy*
Texas, *John Spragins*

Travel Editor, Sunset Magazine
Larry Smith

Executive Editor, Sunset Books
David E. Clark

First Printing October 1972
Copyright ©Lane Magazine & Book Company,
Menlo Park, California.
First Edition 1972. World rights reserved. No part of
this publication may be reproduced by any
mechanical, photographic, or electronic process, or
in the form of a phonographic recording, nor may it
be stored in a retrieval system, transmitted, or
otherwise copied for public or private use without
prior written permission from the publisher.
Library of Congress No. 72-77138. Title
No. 376-05111-6. Lithographed in the United States.

Contents

Land of Enchantment

Embossed into the top of every license plate issued in the state of New Mexico is a proud slogan: "Land of Enchantment." Although few Southwesterners would deny New Mexico's claim to such a motto, many would feel that the label should be stretched to apply to the entire Southwest as well. For in its totality, this is truly an enchanting land.

The magic spell stems from several qualities distinctive to the region.

In part, the enchantment comes from the stunning spaciousness of a wide-open land, spreading to horizons beyond the horizon. Part of the attraction is the vibrant coloring of the landscape, shading from red to purple and varying with the moods of the sky or the angle of the sun, sometimes amplified by flaming sunsets that carry fiery colors into the sky. Part of the fascination also lies in the dramatic variety of the landforms, carved and shaped by wind and water into immense rock sculptures or deep clefts in the earth.

The Southwest is a land of astonishing contrasts and contradictions: of flowers as tiny as pinheads and waxy blossoms as big as soup bowls; ungainly saguaros and great gardens of spring wildflowers. Bone-white desert dunes lie only a few miles from snow-white mountain summits; dry river beds come to life with the savage roar of flooding waters; intimate pockets of shade offer shelter to jack rabbits waiting out the desert sun. Here the silent ruins of prehistoric shelters stand next door to mechanized air-conditioned homes; the oldest towns in the nation sit alongside the newest subdivisions; and modern abstract canvases are on exhibit near locations of prehistoric rock paintings.

A many-branched organ pipe cactus stretches tall above a hillside ablaze with spring wildflowers in southern Arizona. Beautifully adapted to the aridity of the desert, cactus store water during dry periods, and wildflowers turn to seed to escape the relentless summer sun.

Ever-present is a sobering sense of timelessness. Here lies exposed the skeleton of the earth itself, rock that existed two-hundred billion years before life appeared on the planet and fossilized trees that flourished in long-gone swamps some two-hundred million years ago. The bones of dinosaurs and, later, of primitive man stand revealed, exposed by erosion and the patient pecking of archeologists. And in the milliseconds on the cosmic clock, man's recent works stand, crumbling but preserved by the dry air. Hundreds of ruins, spanning thousands of years of man's occupancy, are scattered throughout the Southwest: gaping walls of prehistoric cave dwellings, the dissolved adobes of the first pueblos, toppled stonework of forgotten Spanish missions, and, of more recent vintage, the gaunt remains of U.S. Army forts and the splintering woodwork and rusting tin of ghost towns.

For many Southwesterners the attraction is unquestionably the climate—the nine-month summer—that frees them from the tyrannies of winter. Except for the simmering heat of midsummer midafternoons, the long, sunny season encourages golfers, boating enthusiasts, hikers, and rockhounds to venture forth at a time when the rest of the country is shivering from the cold. Crops are raised, harvested, and marketed well before the ground in the Middle West has warmed up enough for planting. Baseball and football players train for the coming season in open-air, winter camps. Even in summer the Southwesterners know how to relax in the presence of the enervating heat. The fine Latin tradition of *poco tiempo* (of taking it easy, of savoring the siesta) is universally understood in the Southwest. Even the energized Yankees have learned to slow down during the heat of the day. The relaxed

Gawky young burrowing owls stand wide-eyed in the sunlight. Usually these predators spend the day deep in a rodent's cool tunnel, emerging only at nightfall to hunt.

*Migrating sand dunes break like frozen waves against the base of a
mountain range in southern Colorado. The dramatic grandeur of such
scenic contrasts is part of the everyday experience of Southwesterners.*

pace of life contributes to an openness and friendliness that travelers
accept with appreciation.

How far east or west does the Southwest stretch? The answer
depends on where the question is asked. To the Texan the hub of the
Southwest may be in Dallas or even San Antonio. The Tulsa Chamber of
Commerce advertises on its letterhead that it is "The Heart of the
Greater Southwest." At the other geographic extreme, many residents
of Los Angeles consider their city the magnetic pole of the Southwest.

For this book we have taken as our province a geographic area that
is largely desert, generally treeless and shy in rainfall, that covers
all or part of eight states, spreading west from the High Plains of the

Texas Panhandle to the desert dunes along the Colorado River. Across the north the area reaches into the southern tip of Nevada and the red rock country of southern Utah and Colorado. Along the south it runs below the Mexican border. Within this essentially arid province, isolated mountain ranges rise like islands above a sea of sand and rock. Some of these are forested, some rise above timberline; many are barren from base to summit. Two main rivers course through the land: the Colorado along the western edge and the Rio Grande near the eastern periphery. This area contains a sizable portion of the country's most dramatic scenery, some of the largest sun-drenched cities, immense productive ranches, and a great variety of recreational attractions.

A land of little rain, much of the region lies within the rain-shadow of towering mountain barriers that intercept the moist winds from the Pacific Ocean and the Gulf of Mexico and drain them of their water content. The annual rainfall of about ten inches falls mostly in summer in highly localized downpours, accompanied by crackling thunderstorms. So dry is the desert air that the rain often evaporates before it reaches the ground. A second brief wet season comes in winter, with rain falling in the lowlands and snow blanketing the highlands.

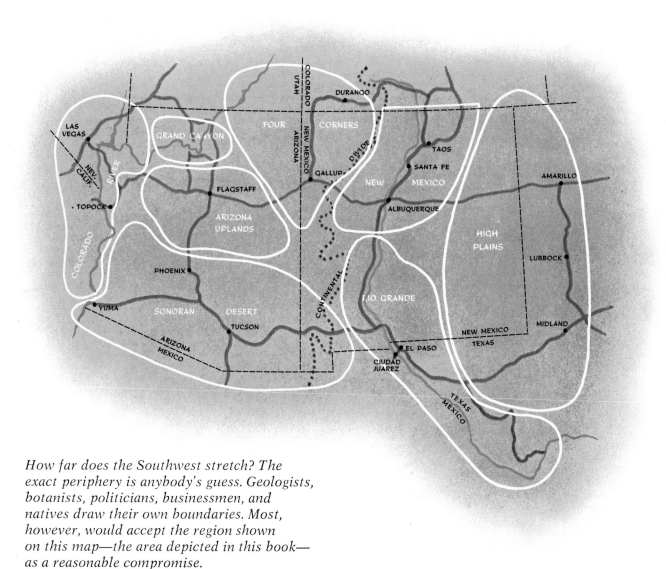

How far does the Southwest stretch? The exact periphery is anybody's guess. Geologists, botanists, politicians, businessmen, and natives draw their own boundaries. Most, however, would accept the region shown on this map—the area depicted in this book— as a reasonable compromise.

Sunset hues, breaking through a blackening sky, illuminate the buttes of Monument Valley like a cosmic stage setting. Such theatrical effects are common to the Southwest, where red earth tones are intensified by the late afternoon rays of the melting sun.

Sunshine is a constancy. The flawless, luminous skies and the searching sun appear through the year, in some areas 365 days without letup. The dry earth radiates solar heat, boosting the air temperature to uncomfortable extremes in summer but holding to temperate levels in winter when most of the rest of the country is chilled by ice and snow.

Native plants and animals are exquisitely evolved to survive in the hot and waterless climate. Plants ration their storage of precious water, restrict their release of water vapor, and rely on their light colored leaves to reflect the sun's rays. Animals go without water, rest in the shade or underground during the heat of day and emerge only in the cool of the night. The birds alone seem impervious to the stern climate. Airborne, they do not suffer from the heat build-up at ground level, and the act of flight cools their bodies in the rush of the wind.

Man has lived in the Southwest for thousands of years. His bones have been unearthed with those of extinct beasts of early geologic time. Descendants of a much later era established settlements in caves, along watercourses, and on the shores of lakes long since turned to sand dunes. Even later, the pueblo dwellers built homes of rock and mud and developed sophisticated farming cultures in the river valleys. Their present-day descendants still live in some of these ancient settlements.

The venturing Spaniards chased the dream of gold here four centuries ago, founded permanent settlements as outposts of Imperial Spain, and converted many of the Indians to a quasi-Christianity, which many still practice along with their ancient naturalistic rites. For four hundred years, the Church has served a vital role throughout the Southwest, and today, the presence of little chapels with flower-decked cemeteries in every town and an ongoing round of religious celebrations attest to its ageless vitality.

Indians and Mexicans lived together in uneasy harmony for two centuries before the Americans arrived in the 1800s. The "Anglos" are thus newcomers in a tri-racial pageant, but in their relatively short term of residency, they have made their mark on the productivity and livability of the region.

Wherever water is brought to the fertile soil, the Southwest blossoms. Great cities develop and crops blanket the river valleys. But because water cannot be piped to every corner of the province or pumped from subterranean reservoirs in every section, most of the Southwest is still thinly populated, primitive, and wild. As one of the nation's last remaining frontiers, the area is likely to remain free and open for a long time—providing it is not exploited beyond its limits or polluted by circumstances of urban growth.

The partisan Southwesterner is not blind to the bleaker aspects of his chosen environment, but he is bewitched by its presence. As one Southwestern writer expressed it, "The arid Southwest has always been too strong, too indomitable for some people. Those who can stand it have had to learn that man does not modify the country—it transforms him, deeply."

The enduring geometry of prehistoric irrigation ditches, ceremonial pits, and masonry walls attest to man's long presence in the Southwest.

Majestic river canyons follow sinuous courses through the land. Cut by the silt-laden rivers, ever-deepening gorges are walled with towering cliffs, buttes, spires, and temples carved out of the not-so-solid rock by the power of running water.

The Sonoran Desert

A land of haunting beauty, limitless horizons . . .
home of giant cactus, bright carpets
of wildflowers . . . haven for wandering dunes

A strange and lonely land, a place of mystery and violent extremes, of sun-baked stillness, the Sonoran Desert exerts a pull that draws men to its hypnotic beauty.

In its natural state, the lonely desert stretches in shimmering emptiness to the far purple hills. Around its horizons stand boldly sculptured mountains, shaped by the abrasive action of wind and water. Its soil reveals itself in bizarre reds, browns, blacks, and yellows that become transformed by the haze of distance into magentas, blues, and purples.

Large sections of the desert are untouched by man's handiwork. No windbreaks limit the horizon, no farmhouses or windmills catch the eye, no crops cover the land. The feeling of isolation is intensified by the profound stillness that makes even the slightest sound seem important —the faint scrabbling of a lizard or a bird in the dry scrub, the swish of wings in the night, the whisper of a warm breeze that comes from nowhere and goes nowhere.

Long before the rest of the West awakens, the desert announces the arrival of spring. Carpets of verbena color the sandy washes, orange poppies blaze over the hills, and tamarisks open like puffs of pink smoke. The whiplike ocotillos break out with tassels of red, yuccas hold their snowy plumes aloft, and the cactus display exquisitely formed, waxy flowers. The show does not last long, for summer also comes early and turns its unrelenting heat upon the plants.

The desert is unforgiving to those who break its rules. But man has learned to tame its harshness and put the land to practical uses. Since before the birth of Christ, man has been living on the desert, extracting a

frugal existence from its plants, animals, and insects. Prehistoric desert dwellers living near the rivers diverted water to irrigate crops of maize, beans, and melons, and built cities of adobe and stone that have stood for a thousand years. These early people abandoned their cities and crops for unknown reasons five centuries ago—they may have been driven out by drought, land failure, or warfare—but their descendants are still living in the drylands of Arizona and New Mexico.

Despite being a latecomer to the desert, the white man has made his mark. In less than a century, he has reclaimed thousands of acres of wasteland by irrigation and made the fertile soil burgeon with crops of cotton, melons, and lettuce. In the towns, vacation colonies, and resorts, year-round residents live in air-conditioned comfort, and winter visitors flock to the lowlands to soak up sunshine, to boat on the rivers and the man-made lakes, and to explore the wildlands.

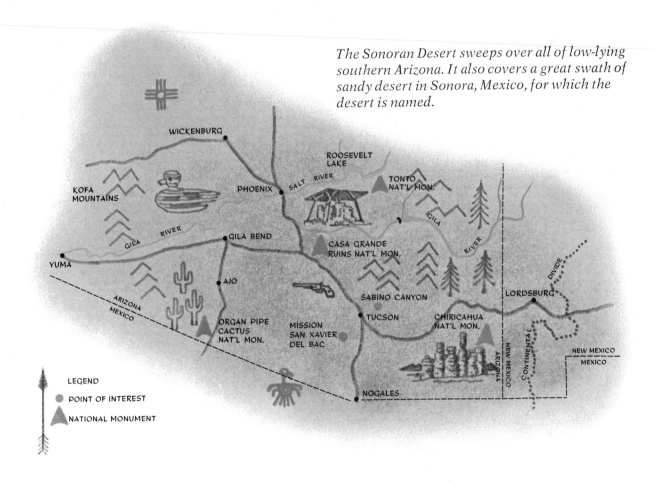

The Sonoran Desert sweeps over all of low-lying southern Arizona. It also covers a great swath of sandy desert in Sonora, Mexico, for which the desert is named.

Arizona's only stand of native palms grows in a deep cleft in the Kofa Mountains, northeast of Yuma. These rare palms flourish in an earthquake fault in the craggy, volcanic mountains.

The Restless Dunes

*Driest of the dry, the ancient beaches and beds
of prehistoric lakes are blown about by the
powerful desert winds and sculptured into great
mountainous dunes that stretch for miles.
Ever on the march, the dunes are blown forward
until they reach an insurmountable barrier,
perhaps a mountain range, and there they live
out their restless days. Where the sands
threaten to engulf highways and croplands,
conventional snow fencing (below) is often used
to restrain the migratory dunes.*

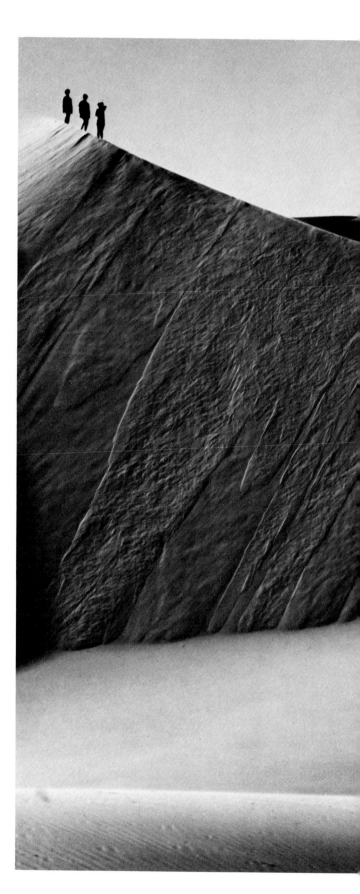

Mesquite

Yucca elata

Saguaro

Mammillaria

Nama demissum & Monoptilon bellioides

Euphorbia albomarginata

Hedgehog cactus

Ocotillo

Miraculous Garden

Following the first rains, desert plants burst into bloom. Cactus blossom in clusters and in garlands of bright, waxy flowers; the ocotillo breaks out a showy red tassel. Some blooms are barely visible—"belly flowers" are so tiny a dozen would fit on a penny.

Hibiscus denudatus

Encelia farinosa

20

Poppies blanket the hills in Tonto National Monument, near Roosevelt Lake. After a few days of glory, the plants turn to seed to escape the scorching summer heat.

21

Armed for Adversity

To survive the climatic extremes in the desert, where temperatures range from below freezing to 120°, native plants have evolved a variety of defenses. As a protection against the burning sun, plants rely on light-colored leaves and stems that reflect sunlight, small leaves that reduce transpiration, pores that close during the heat of the day. The spines on cactus (left)—reflecting sunlight, trapping moving air, and helping cool the plants—allow it to survive and flourish in the furnacelike temperatures. The sharp barbs also protect the plants from foraging animals and provide sanctuary for small rodents and birds, such as the mourning dove (right) resting gingerly in a bower of needle-sharp cholla spines.

Denizens of the Desert

Linked together in the food chain, the kit fox and its prey, the abundant jack rabbit, rely on their oversized ears for their deadly game of hide and seek. As a mainstay of the diet of many predators, the jack rabbit is born already on the defensive. The baby hares arrive fully furred and open-eyed—ready to hop to safety.

Like desert plants, animals have also adapted to the heat and lack of water. To avoid the sun, they snooze during the day in burrows or in shaded cover and only move around in the coolness of night. To satisfy their moisture needs, plant-eaters feed on the vegetation, taking in water stored in the plants. The meat-eaters then consume the plant-eaters and quench their thirst with the blood of their prey. One of the most perfect examples of adaptive living is the agile, feisty kangaroo rat that never touches a drop of water in its life. It makes its own supply by combining the hydrogen in food with inhaled oxygen.

SONORAN DESERT   **25**

The Burgeoning Desert

Near Gila Bend thousands of cattle and sheep are wintered on the open range. Cattle ranchers raise Brahmans and cross them with domestic strains; many are used for the rodeo circuit. More than 90,000 acres of desert land have been put under cultivation, irrigated with water diverted from the Colorado and Gila rivers. Farmers grow alfalfa, grain (right), cotton, melons, citrus, lettuce, grapes, and dates. Some of Arizona's highest yielding cotton acreages lie along the Gila River bed, producing as much as three bales to the acre. Because of the favorable winter climate, warm-weather crops, such as citrus (at left is early grapefruit crate label), are harvested in the dead of winter, well ahead of the rest of the country.

Storm over the Saguaros

A darkening sky heralds the approach of a storm over a forest of saguaro cactus baking under a relentless sun in Organ Pipe National Monument. The giant plants soak up the life-giving rain through their extensive roots and store the water in their tall fluted columns.

Man-Made Crater

Since 1854 copper miners have been excavating an immense cavity in the desert near Ajo. A sobering spectacle, it is now as large as a meteor crater, 800 feet deep and nearly a mile across. Electric trains ascend spiraling terraces to bring out the ore, 63 tons to a carload. Started during the uncertain years when southern Arizona was still a part of Mexico, the mine was harassed by Apaches and later by Mexican troops. This vast pit is only one of Arizona's several copper mines which collectively produce the bulk of the nation's ore.

Man is not the only digger in the desert. The bright-eyed, industrious ground squirrel, though working on a smaller scale, manages to move his share of desert soil.

January Outing

Opportunities for outdoor living persist through eight months of the year and die down only during the scorching months of summer. Even then, some leather-skinned desert dwellers head for the golf courses, boating lakes (right), landscaped parks, and riding stables. However, most prefer to venture outdoors in the balmy dead of winter. A bright January day is perfect for seeking out the refreshing sight of a body of water. Riders (left) trot over dry brush on their way to Roosevelt Lake; those above canter along a bridle path built next to an irrigation canal in Phoenix.

Rising Phoenix

One-third of Arizona's population lives within the boundaries of mushrooming Phoenix, which spreads over a wide expanse of territory and washes halfway up the slopes of distinctive Camelback Mountain. Rising on the site of an ancient Indian settlement—hence the name "Phoenix"—in the 1860s, it started out as a hay camp to supply cavalry horses at nearby Fort McDowell. The camp grew slowly, even though designated the territorial capital in 1889. However, completion in 1911 of the Theodore Roosevelt Dam on the Salt River brought irrigation water to the area and spurred the city's growth. World War II triggered further development with a concentration of aircraft industries and Air Force training bases, causing the population to double and re-double.

Remnant of the original 13th-century settlement is this excavated section of irrigation canal, constructed by the Hohokam (see page 40) and abandoned about 1350. This was part of an extensive system that tapped the Salt River for water. When white settlers moved here five centuries later, they re-dug the ancient canals and built a modern irrigation complex around the prehistoric system.

Desert Living for a New Day

*Something in the clear air, the honest sunlight, and the sculptured forms
of cliff and eroded plain seems to kindle imaginative desert architecture.
Among the many examples of inspired work in the area are two outstanding
structures not far from Phoenix: Taliesin West, designed by the late
Frank Lloyd Wright, and the studios of his illustrious student, Paolo Soleri.
Taliesin West (above), a school for practicing architects and students,
embodies in its dramatic design many of the concepts of the great master
of naturalistic architecture.*

*In the desert north of Scottsdale,
a radical concept in city design is
taking shape under the visionary
guidance of Soleri, whose remarkable
studio (far right) is partly dug into
the earth and domed with perforated
concrete. Soleri believes that the life
of city dwellers can be made more
meaningful by building new cities in
the form of mountain-sized structures,
a mile or more in height, such as
the models at right, standing in the
midst of open space.*

Soleri's studio, living and working quarters for the architect and his apprentices, displays the distinctive Soleri sculptures, bells.

Water Playground

A power boat cuts a swath through the sun-struck waters of Canyon Lake (left), one of a chain of reservoirs along the path of the Salt River near Phoenix. The series of dams that harnesses the river for irrigation and power has created a 60-mile waterway for desert sailors, motor-boatsmen, and excursionists. One of the most novel desert water sports is artificial surfing (right), practiced near Phoenix, where scores of bronzed surfers ride 5-foot breakers, mechanically generated every 80 seconds.

Prehistoric Farmers

Beginning about the time of Christ, ancestors of the Indians now living in the Gila River Valley irrigated and farmed the rich desert lands. Living in walled settlements built of rammed earth or masonry, the Hohokam—the Ancient Ones—tapped the Gila River system starting in 700 A.D. and ultimately built 200 miles of irrigation canals some 25 feet wide and 15 feet deep. For fourteen centuries they peacefully raised crops of maize (corn), beans, pumpkins, and cotton. Then, for unknown reasons, they abandoned their settlements around 1400 and vanished from history. Some of the prehistoric tribes lived in cliff dwellings near the valley farmlands. A fine example is in Tonto National Monument (below), near Roosevelt Lake. This cliffside apartment was occupied by Salado Indians 600 years ago.

A most unusual ruin of the early farming communities is the Casa Grande,
a multi-story adobe apartment and watchtower south of Phoenix, built
in 1350 by Pueblo Indians who had moved in with the Hohokam. Abandoned
since 1450, the remains are now protected from the rain by a metal
umbrella.

White Dove of the Desert

Resplendent Mission San Xavier del Bac, south of Tucson, is a handsome reminder of the time when the area was a bustling outpost of the Spanish empire. Founded in 1692, the original chapel was destroyed by Apaches. The present church, built between 1783 and 1797, is one of the oldest continually used churches in the nation. Its incomplete tower is said to have been left unfinished so the padres could continually ask for funds to "complete" the structure. Although the mission is operated by the Dominican order, it was established by the Jesuits, whose insignia (left) is an ornate feature of the façade. Each spring during Tucson Festival Week, fireworks light up the sky above Mission San Xavier del Bac to celebrate its founding.

Ideal Habitats for Plants and Animals

Showcase of desert living for both plants and animals, the Arizona-Sonora Desert Museum (just west of Tucson) offers both a first-class zoo and a fine demonstration garden. Some residents of the zoo, such as this prowling bobcat, are sequestered in accurately simulated habitats; others, such as the desert tortoise (left), can be met person to person.

A concrete ramada shelters a lounging terrace in the botanical garden.
Plant materials on display are natives and desert-tolerant exotics, chosen
and groomed by Sunset *Magazine.*

Canyon Oases

The sight and sound of running water is a refreshing contrast for desert dwellers. Accessible canyons and arroyos coursed by live streams, such as these two different oases near Tucson, are cherished retreats. Aravaipa Creek (left) meanders quietly through a sandy arroyo. In rocky Sabino Canyon (below), water tumbles among boulders or eddies into sand-beached pools—a favorite haunt of young people.

Apache Bastion

A natural maze of eroded lava, the Chiricahua Mountains in southeastern Arizona once sheltered raiding bands of Apache Indians that terrorized the border country in the 1880s. Fighting against the white man's taking over their ancestral lands, the marauders were finally subdued in 1886 when their chief, Geronimo, surrendered.

Poised on top of a pinnacle in Chiricahua National Monument, an immense rock balancing precariously appears ready to topple into the canyon below—as it well may, after another million years or so of erosion.

Up the Colorado

Marine boulevard to desert wilderness . . .

jagged mountains and reedy thickets . . .

man-made reservoirs behind a series of dams

On the final leg of its almost 1,500 mile run from the Rockies to the Gulf of California, the Colorado River snakes a twisting course through the desert, passing inside deep desolate canyons, widening out occasionally into reed-rimmed lagoons, or disappearing in the vast reaches of inland seas created by a series of dams. Along its lonely way, the river passes few major settlements, a half-dozen river crossings, and a few historic river ports dating from the 1860s.

The Colorado has been a life giving resource to man ever since the aborigines camped along its banks. It provided a freeway for water-borne travelers, a source of food, and an abundant supply of reeds and sedges useful in making rafts, mats, baskets, weapons, and shelters. The Yuma Indians, who lived near the present city of Yuma, learned to divert some of the river flow into irrigation canals to support crops of maize and beans.

Today an immense complex of settling basins and canals taps the Colorado for irrigation and domestic water supply, with much of the agriculture and most of the major cities of southern California and southwestern Arizona depending on water from the river. The Colorado also offers recreational opportunities. Its banks are edged with bait shops, campgrounds, and marinas, and the expanse of water invites fishermen, water-skiers, or boatsmen to explore the side canyons that zigzag off the great reservoirs.

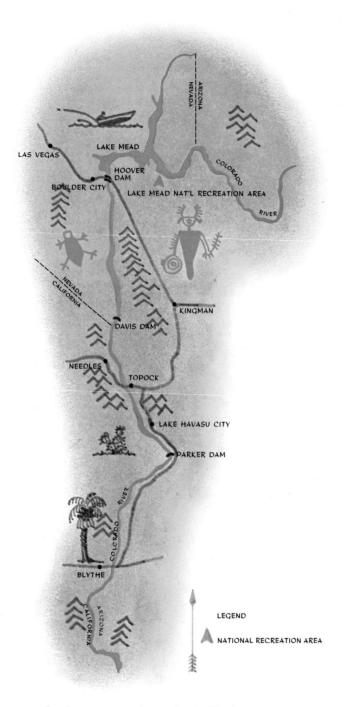

The river was named in 1604 by Spanish explorers who encountered it at flood tide, when its silt-laden water was stained a chocolate brown. Rio Colorado—red river—they called it. Now running clear, except when muddied by flash floods, the river retained its ruddy hue ("too thick to drink, too thin to plow") until the building of the dams that cause the silt to settle to the bottom.

Before the great dams were constructed, the Colorado enjoyed a half-century of waterborne commerce. Miniature Mississippi paddlewheelers sailed from a makeshift port on the Gulf of California to Black Canyon, the beginning of the Grand Canyon and the headwaters of navigation.

The first steamer to penetrate to the Black Canyon was a 54-foot steel vessel that was built in Philadelphia, disassembled, shipped piecemeal across the Isthmus, and reassembled at the mouth of the Colorado in 1857. The clumsy, underpowered steamer ran aground several times and was nearly capsized in rapids, but it did successfully negotiate a voyage to Black Canyon and back. It operated on the river for three years, probably as a barge. One night in 1860 it slipped its anchorage at Pilot Knob (in Arizona) and disappeared. Its rusted ribs were found on dry land in Sonora, Mexico, 70 years later by a survey party.

On its way south to the Gulf of California, the Colorado River below the Grand Canyon is interrupted by three major dams that change the flowing river into immense desert lakes.

Found in isolated groves in southern Nevada and northern Arizona, Bristlecone pines are the oldest trees on earth. Some were 1,500 years of age when Moses led his people out of Egypt. To survive in adverse soil and climate, the trees grow rapidly in favorable years, go near-dormant during very dry cycles. The twisted trunks, 90 per cent dead wood, are kept alive by a slim strip of bark.

Up the Lazy River

On secret lakes beneath
towering crags, boaters can
explore the gentle (current
moves at 5 knots) Colorado
River below the big dams.
Motorboats furrow the water
all through the year. Canoes
càn be paddled into the
shallow side channels,
inaccessible to power boats.
The inboard cruiser above is
sweeping past Picacho;
canoers (right) are silently
probing the narrow offshoots
in the Devils Elbow section
of Topock Gorge.

Messages from the Past

Enduring records of man's 20,000-year presence along the Colorado River are the scattered rock paintings of animals, hunters, and puzzling symbols (above). Most unusual of the desert records is the immense cluster of intaglios (far right), first sighted from the air in 1938. The large figures (180 feet long) depict deer, antelope, and Indian hunters. These carvings are estimated to be at least 200 years old. Drawings show Bighorn sheep, which still roam the rocky hills along the Colorado River.

London Bridge on the Colorado

Unbelievable sight on the river is a stone bridge, formerly traversing the Thames in England, now arching across a dredged lagoon at Lake Havasu City. Not the "falling down" bridge of the nursery rhyme, this lineal descendant was built in 1831 and dedicated with great fanfare. Too narrow for present-day London traffic, the old bridge was sold to the desert community for 2½ million dollars. Transported here numbered stone by numbered stone, it was reconstructed and opened to the public in 1971. Surprisingly, it fits well into the meticulously planned desert community.

Brisk warm winds of April bring twin-hulled catamarans to the lagoon for the annual battle of the "cats" on Lake Havasu. The regatta attracts 200 sailors.

Lake Mead Area

A solitary sailboat explores the waters around a solitary island in the midst of wide-open Lake Mead, one of the world's largest man-made reservoirs. Backed up behind Hoover Dam, the many-armed lake offers inland sailors an unparalleled opportunity to explore the desert by boat or to cast for strapping large-mouth bass. Below the dam the spectacular Black Canyon of the Colorado (right) stretches 20 miles downstream.

River Be Dammed

Where once a roiling river ran, long serpentine lakes now stretch for miles, backed up behind a series of dams. The restrained current runs placidly, shimmering in the moonlight or mirroring the hot skies of noon. Tamed to provide power or irrigation needs, the water level of the Colorado is manipulated to supply the needs of farmers and industries hundreds of miles away. Generally, the water level may vary a foot or two over a twenty-four hour period. Sometimes the draw-down is even more drastic, leaving the shoreline rimmed with miles of jig-sawed mud flats.

Starboard to Cactus

A few miles inland from the Colorado River, sand sailors tack across the smooth playas near Las Vegas. Like their waterborne cousins, these land yachts can be spilled by a change in the wind or inept dressing of the sails— a dusty and abrasive happening that leaves its mark on the unhappy sportsman. Sand sailing has been a popular desert sport off and on since the 1890s. Nearby on both sides of the river are groves of the many-limbed Joshua trees (Yucca brevifolia), bizarre members of the lily family that live 70 to 100 years. Tradition has it that the plants were named by the Mormons for the Biblical patriarch who guided the Israelites out of Canaan. The wildly waving arms supposedly directed the Mormons to a safe path across the desert.

Mustangs on the Run

Galloping over the desert in southern Nevada, a string of wild mustangs races for safety. The wary animals have been banished by ranchers, shot by hunters, and slaughtered for dog food. Fifty years ago a million wild horses roamed the western ranges; now only an estimated 17,000 survive, sequestered in a few federal ranges. Ever on the move, stallions ride herd on harems of mares and send them galloping to safety at the slightest whiff of danger. The lead mare chooses the escape route and the stallions race along behind, neighing and nipping at the flanks of stragglers. Stallions battle each other for control of the harems—to the complete indifference of the mares and their offsprings.

Cattle Country

In southern Nevada cowpokes still ride the range in time-honored ways, driving small herds across the sparse land and rounding up the crafty animals that play hide and seek in the arroyos. In winter, temperatures often drop below freezing at night, forcing a rancher to smash the ice cap on the watering tank so the stock can quench their thirst in the chilly dawn.

The Grand Canyon

Geologic history of the planet on view . . .

vistas that stun the senses . . . depths

to explore, a roiling river to run

"**N**o matter how far you have wandered hitherto, or how many famous gorges and valleys you have seen, this one, the Grand Canyon of the Colorado will seem as novel to you, as unearthly in the color and grandeur and quantity of its architecture, as if you had found it after death, on some other star." So wrote naturalist John Muir, after visiting the South Rim in the 1890s. Muir eloquently sums up the emotional response—utter disbelief in the incredible size of it all—aroused in the traveler when he first comes upon this vast spectacle.

Whatever humbling effect the spectacle may have, the Grand Canyon is, in essence, simply the supreme example of the shaping power of running water. For millions of years, the silt-laden Colorado River has rasped a channel into a slowly rising landscape, exposing one layer after another of the planet's crust, until it has revealed literally the inside of the earth, shiny black rock so ancient there is no clue as to its origin.

Primitive man visited the depths of the Canyon to hunt, mine salt, or collect berries and medicinal plants, but few apparently found it a hospitable place to live. White men first encountered the gorge in the 1540s when Spanish conquistadores stumbled upon it in their quest for the legendary cities of gold.

The first Americans to approach the Grand Canyon explored it up-river from the Gulf of California in 1857. A waterborne expedition under Lieutenant J. C. Ives steamed as far as Black Canyon, the western gate of the Grand Canyon, and explored a little farther into the Canyon before turning back. Ives was depressed by this "profitless locality" and predicted that "It seems by nature that the Colorado River, along the greater portion of its lonely and majestic way, shall be forever unvisited and undisturbed."

Despite Ives' pessimistic prophesy, a few years later the "greater portion" of the "lonely and majestic" Colorado was explored by a flotilla under the command of a one-armed artillery Major, John Wesley Powell,

whose name is immortalized in the immense lake that today backs up behind Glen Canyon Dam. Powell's expedition passed down the length of the Grand Canyon in a disaster-ridden voyage that revealed this unknown land could be penetrated. Two years later Powell returned with a better-equipped party. In 1875 he published a report on the expeditions that stirred wide interest in the Grand Canyon and prompted scientists, prospectors, and tourists to visit the Canyon wilderness.

In the decades that followed the Powell survey, the Grand Canyon was explored, prospected, mined, festooned with cable cars, laced with a network of steep trails, and dotted with resorts, hotels, and wayside gardens. In fact, the region was being so energetically exploited that official steps were taken to sequester the area in a federal park. Efforts began in the 1870s; it was not until 1919 that it became a National Park.

To the present-day traveler, Grand Canyon National Park is divided into four components: the populous South Rim, easiest to reach and closest to major highways and cities; the North Rim, higher in elevation than the opposite rim and less crowded because of its remoteness and its short season; the Inner Canyon, a deep gorge within the Grand Canyon and accessible only by trail; and the Colorado River itself, a turbulent watercourse, favored by an ever-increasing horde of river-runners.

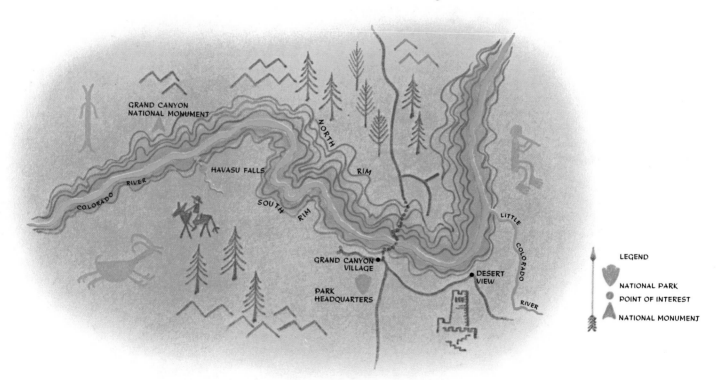

The convoluted course of the Colorado River gorge decisively separates Grand Canyon National Park into two different worlds: a North Rim and a South Rim, 9 miles apart as the crow flies or 200 miles by road.

Late afternoon sunlight intensifies the well-defined shapes and brilliant colors of the Grand Canyon and emphasizes the overwhelmingly vertical scale of the awesome gorge.

Down into the Depths

For most visitors to the South Rim, the first overwhelming view of the
Grand Canyon is the overlook at Mather Point (right), 3,400 feet above the
Colorado River. Across the chasm the buttes and battlements of the North
Rim recede to the distant Kaibab Plateau. Cutting 19 miles northward
into the Plateau is Bright Angel Canyon, an impressive gorge in its own
right. Trails connect the North and South rims and descend by an endless
series of switchbacks, steeper on the precipitous wall of the South Rim
than on the stepped wall to the north. Blasé burros plod methodically down
the memorized route, inconsiderately stopping once in a while at the brink
of eternity to admire the view, oblivious to the nerves of their
timorous riders.

South Rim Moods

An ever-changing rainbow, the view from the South Rim varies according to the time of day, time of year, and kind of weather. The warm rays of sunrise or sunset enrich the pinks, reds, and purples; the lowering clouds of a stormy sky turn the landscape to varying shades of blue. In winter, snow piled up on the South Rim softens the sharp angularity with a frosting of white.

Canyon within the Canyon

Within the Grand Canyon itself is a second canyon, the V-shaped Inner Gorge, cut 1,000 feet into the rock by the grinding Colorado River.

79

High on the North Rim

The deeply incised North Rim offers a scape different from that at the South Rim. Vast side canyons, great amphitheaters, and monumental islands of rock, standing free of the rim, provide a dramatic foreground for views into the Canyon and beyond. Probing into the Canyon are long promontories—some with walls so thin that they have been pierced by wind and frost erosion, as exemplified by Angels Window (below) near Cape Royal. Because of its elevation, the North Rim feels the grip of winter earlier and later than the opposite rim, 1,000 feet lower. Late in May the Bright Angel Trail is still edged with snow at the trail head near Bright Angel Lodge.

Spectacular North Rim

The most awesome vertical drop in Grand Canyon's national park area is the overlook at Toroweap Point (left), where the walls of the Canyon narrow to within hailing distance, although they are actually several hundred miles apart by road. This is one of the few sites within the Canyon where it is possible to see the Colorado River from the top of the cliffs, 3,000 giddy feet above the churning water. A drama of another kind occurs in fall when the north country blazes with aspen gold. At 7,000 feet the North Rim duplicates the life zones of northern Canada and supports great forests of aspen, royal oak, and conifers. Looking down, the viewer sees a startling contrast—desert at the river's edge. Each 1,000 feet of descent is equivalent to 300 miles of travel to the south in terms of plant and animal habitats.

Surprises at the Water's Edge

For those who explore the canyon within the Canyon by boat, this narrow slot of a world is graced with intimate surprises: desert dunes at the mouth of Kanab Creek, patches of pretty but poisonous jimsonweed, an inquisitive wild burro peering from a rocky sanctuary, flights of avocets streaking up-canyon.

Challenges of the Canyon Gorges

The canyon depths challenge those with a venturesome spirit to test their skills against the seething rapids or to search out the secrets of the side gorges. The boatsman tumbling through Lava Falls (below) is entrusting his all to a staunch dory, considered by some to be more controllable than the bulbous rafts favored by most river runners. For persevering hikers, innumerable side canyons offer once-in-a-lifetime rewards. An excursion might lead to a rocky labyrinth, such as the corkscrew trench that clear-running Deer Creek has cut through the brown sandstone, or to a dip in the aquamarine pools at Havasu Creek (left).

Arizona Uplands

*Land of the purple sage, of ponderosas and
golden aspens . . . sycamore-filled canyons . . .
snow sports for desert dwellers*

Those who picture Arizona as all sun and cactus are in for a refreshing surprise when they first encounter the mountainous province, dominated by the looming San Francisco Peaks, that stretches across the northern part of the state.

To experience this mountain world is to have one's senses assaulted. The eye catches vistas of purple, sage-covered hills and mesas, the grandeur of red-walled gorges and arroyos, and the flash of autumn splendor. The aroma of campfire and fireplace smoke hangs in the air, the wild song of the coyote choir salutes the dawn and the dusk.

Arizona's Upland is a concentration of scenic variety ranging from high, barren mesas to irregular stands of juniper and dark forests of ponderosa pine. Encompassed within this Upland and its approaches from the desert below are forests of petrified wood, cinder cones, a waterfall higher than Niagara, a moon-style meteor crater, and several miniature Grand Canyons.

This is high country, much of it above a mile in elevation. In bracing contrast to the arid lands below, the Uplands are favored with a cooler summer and a real, no-nonsense winter season. Snow starts falling before Christmas and blankets the higher elevations until Memorial Day. The close proximity of this snowy world to the tropical lowlands offers a recreational opportunity that both uplanders and lowlanders enthusiastically exploit. Mountain dwellers, driving down-canyon to thaw out in the desert, pass lowlanders hurrying up to play in the snow.

For thousands of years, this favored land has been a friendly habitat for man. Remnants of prehistoric settlements are clustered around old watercourses and ponds. Descendants of the Ancient Ones still live in mountain villages and carry forward tribal customs and ceremonies.

History has swept through the region, leaving behind a record of courage, determination, and occasionally, violence. Conquest of the land often involved conquest of the people who had arrived first. Old army posts and forts remain from the bloody years of warfare between white men and the Indians. A scattering of gravestones and historical markers recall a later period when cowboys and sheepmen battled over grazing rights. Many of the episodes and characters involved in this embittered conflict have been dramatized in the widely popular novels by Zane Grey, who lived in the Tonto Basin.

Mining towns, both dead and alive, cling to the rocky, ore-rich mountainsides. Some of them evolved into vigorous modern cities. Prescott, for a time the capital of the Territory, is a thriving mining and vacation center. Flagstaff, the unofficial capital of this mountain province, stands at the gateway to the Grand Canyon and a wide vacationland. It is the site of outstanding museums and observatories and the locale for the famous Indian Pow Wow, which brings tribal representatives from all over the Southwest to celebrate a three-day jamboree each Fourth of July.

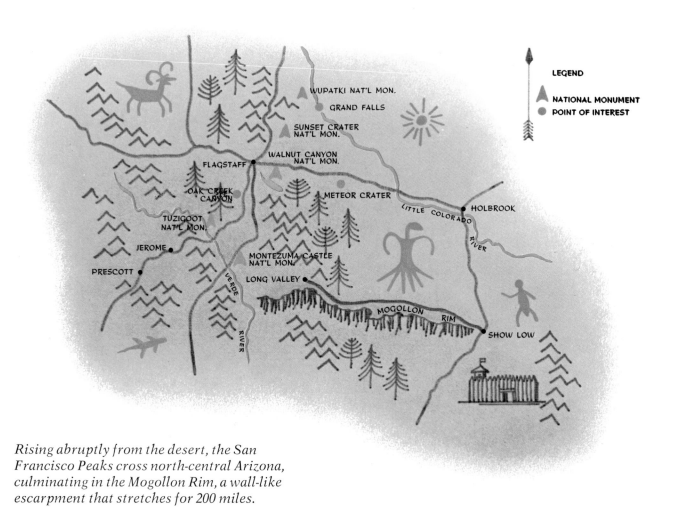

Rising abruptly from the desert, the San Francisco Peaks cross north-central Arizona, culminating in the Mogollon Rim, a wall-like escarpment that stretches for 200 miles.

*Always startling when seen in full scale for the first time, the brilliant
cliffs of Oak Creek Canyon provide a dramatic introduction to the highlands
ahead. As the canyon ascends, earth colors change from white to orange
to red, and in the dying sun take on a fiery hue.*

Gateway to the Uplands

In its climb from the desert to the highlands, Oak Creek Canyon sweeps through sagebrush country brightened with sycamore-lined washes, then passes through a spacious array of erosion-carved buttes (below). Near the settlement of Sedona, a side road leads to the dramatic Chapel of the Holy Cross (left), boldly outlined against its red rock background. The chapel, built in 1956 as a family memorial, is open to the public. Visitors are requested to enter quietly and to leave cameras outside.

High Spirits in the Highlands

Parades, ceremonies, and rodeos bring together the Indians of the Uplands for periodic celebrations. A famous feature of Flagstaff's annual All-Indian Pow Wow is the parade of Zuni women, serenely carrying pots balanced on their heads. Another important annual event occurs in February when the Hopi Kachina spirits are supposed to come down out of the mountains to reward and admonish the Hopi people. Colorfully costumed dancers, each representing a Kachina spirit, impersonate the supernatural visitors in ceremonial functions. The dancers give the Hopi children beautifully carved, brightly colored, and highly treasured Kachina dolls (above).

Calf-roping is an exciting event at the Annual White Mountain Apache Tribal Fair and Rodeo held in Whiteriver over the Labor Day weekend. This is cattle country, and the rodeo gives the cowboy a chance to test his skills at a favorite sport.

Mining Ghosts

At the mercy of winds and the pitiless sun, scores of abandoned mining towns wither away in the ore-rich mountains. Once a rambunctious copper town of 15,000, Jerome, high on the slopes of Mingus Mountain, boomed from 1876 to 1929 before depletion of the high-grade ores slowed the town down. Most of Jerome's people departed, but an obstinate few—some retired, some working nearby, some catering to tourists—have kept a spark of life in this curious, cliff-hanging community.

Dramatic Earth-Shaping Forces

Two reminders of the fragility of the earth's crust are visible in the high desert east of Flagstaff. An immense crater (above), similar in form to those on the moon (right), was blasted out 50,000 years ago when 10 million tons of meteorites slammed into the earth. A more contemporary force, the shaping power of running water can be witnessed at Grand Falls, where the plunging Little Colorado River flows chocolate brown, dyed by tons of silt washed from the land upriver.

Home of the Aspen Glow

Splashes of scintillating foliage brighten the western slopes of the San Francisco Peaks in autumn when the quaking aspen break out their golden color. Groves of the stately trees line the highways or rim forest ponds in the higher elevations. Linked to the history of the trappers and fur traders, this striking tree has long been rooted in western lore. Its tender bark is appetizing to the beaver, and trappers in the 1840s often looked first for aspen in searching for their prey. In the white bark of the trees, these lonely men sometimes carved sentiments— initials, hearts and arrows, and robust obscenities—that are still visible on an occasional trunk.

Arizona's Desert Alps

*From mid-December into March, deep snows transform the barren
summits of the San Francisco Peaks into a sparkling alpine world,
strikingly different from the balmy desert an hour's drive below.
Wind-driven snow (upper left) shrouds the crest of Humphreys Peak
(12,633 feet), the highest point in the state, and blankets the rocky slopes
of nearby Mount Agassiz (above) with a heavy mantle of skiable snow.
Campgrounds along the road to the summit (left) are cold and deserted;
the dark outlines of the trees contrasting with the snow covering
the ground give the illusion of an etching.*

Haunt of Ancient Man

Early man found this land to his liking and wrested a living from the soil for centuries before moving on to unknown destinations for unknown reasons. The ancient occupants of Tuzigoot (left), near Clarkdale, lived on this ridgetop in a 110-room pueblo and cultivated fertile ground along the Verde River until early in the 1400s. The Indians who lived near tranquil Montezuma Well (above), near Camp Verde, engineered an irrigation system to divert water to their fields. Portions of these old canals still exist.

Zane Grey Country

The forests and valleys of Mogollon Rim country still seem to echo the shots, the stilted curses, and the pounding hooves that enliven the 60-odd adventure novels of Zane Grey, who immortalized this land of the purple sage in purple prose that has been read by millions all over the world.

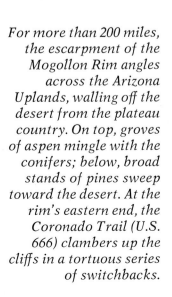

For more than 200 miles, the escarpment of the Mogollon Rim angles across the Arizona Uplands, walling off the desert from the plateau country. On top, groves of aspen mingle with the conifers; below, broad stands of pines sweep toward the desert. At the rim's eastern end, the Coronado Trail (U.S. 666) clambers up the cliffs in a tortuous series of switchbacks.

Four Corners Area

*A fantasy land of sculptured rock, pinnacles,
arches, domes…a painted desert of vibrant colors…
enduring Indian civilizations*

Fanning out from the Four Corners—the only point in the United States where four states (Arizona, New Mexico, Utah, Colorado) meet—is a vast expanse containing some of the most colorful and surprising scenery in the Southwest. A land of desolate beauty, it occupies a great plateau of arid wilderness, broken by mountains and mesas, rocks and rangeland, caves and canyons, fields and forests.

It is a lonely land. Despite the presence of scattered settlements and roving bands of herdsmen, despite the paved roads and the lacework of jeep trails, the over-all impression is of an unoccupied country, the dominant memory is of stillness and peace.

Remarkable on the painted desert is its dramatic, sculptured-sandstone scenery, carved out of the bed of an ancient sea by the patient action of water, wind, and frost. These elements cut deep canyons across the flat surface and exposed the volcanic roots of mountains, pinnacles, buttes, and spires that tower above the level horizon.

Perhaps no scene in the region exceeds the striking landscape of the much photographed Monument Valley. Ever-changing, according to the time of day, the season of the year, or the weather, the great bowl becomes an electrifying spectacle at sundown. The warm rays of the setting sun

turn the red buttes to crimson; the low angle of the sun's rays cast shadows that reach across the level plain for forty-five miles. But the climactic scene does not last long. As the sun sinks, the shadows race across the desert, vanishing the instant the sun drops below the horizon.

Because of its altitude (3,500 to 5,500 feet), the Four Corners area is often covered with light snowfall in winter. The rains fall in summer, usually in intense, localized downpours. The deep blue skies of summer are often filled with great mountains of billowing cumulous clouds which vanish by nightfall. The crystal clear night sky sparkles with a profusion of stars or flares briefly with distant sheet or forked lightning.

The region includes most of the drainage area of the Little Colorado River, as well as sections of the upper Colorado and the San Juan rivers, which have cut deep, twisting courses through the badlands.

The Four Corners area is rich in archeological relics, evidence of an advanced agrarian culture of a thousand years ago. Ancestors of the Indians now living in the desert nestled in cliff houses and farmed the rich soil in the river valleys that twist between towering rock walls. Settlers abandoned their communal apartments in the 1300s, probably because of a prolonged drought, leaving behind thousands of dwellings tucked in the soaring rock, high above the reach of flash floods and hostile raiders.

The fragmentary and tantalizing record of early Indian life is visible in the numerous petroglyphs, pecked into rocks along trails or in hidden recesses, that depict animals, hunters, and symbols of earth and sky.

Archeologists are uncertain what many of these drawings signify. The decorated rock faces may have served as early-day message centers for the Basketmaker Indians who farmed here between 200 and 700 A.D., or the carvings may have been magic symbols to insure good living. Some of the rock pictures are obviously more recent. Those that depict man on horseback would have had to be drawn after the appearance of the Spaniards in the 16th century, for the horse was unknown in the region prior to that time.

This area is also memorable for its present occupants, the Navajos and Hopis, whose distinctive cultures have survived long after those of most North American tribes have all but disappeared.

First on the scene were the Hopis, direct descendants of the original cliff dwellers. By the late 1600s, Navajo nomads had begun to filter in around the established colonies of the Hopis, and by the mid 1800s they had settled extensively in the area. About 132,000 Navajos now live on a 19-million-acre reservation that occupies a substantial portion of the painted desert (in fact, in some quarters the area is still referred to as the Navahoan Desert). This is the largest tribe and the largest reservation in the country. Having retained their pueblo style of existence, the Hopis live on a reservation in the center of the immense Navajo preserve. Although both tribes are adopting some of the white man's ways, they steadfastly retain many of their tribal customs, rites, and crafts.

Droll Goblin Valley

The eroded badlands of Utah's Goblin Valley
can be as bizarre as the visitor's imagination
will allow. For the very fanciful, the valley is
peopled with goblins, space creatures, and
fairy tale characters. For the more literal-
minded, it is an array of pedestal-mounted
creations naturally carved from the sandstone.
The formation in the foreground at right can
either be the March Hare or Donald Duck's
bill, depending on the viewing angle. This
ludicrous collection of dome-headed figures
is located north of Hanksville.

Two horsemen silhouetted against a sunlit slope give some idea of the massive scale and unforgettable grandeur of the soaring walls characteristic of the Four Corners area.

A colorful desert area radiates from the Four Corners, the only point in the United States where four states touch boundaries. The region includes within its amoeba-like boundaries some of the most impressive ruins of ancient native cultures and the largest concentration of Indians in the Southwest.

Arches in the Devil's Garden

One of the world's most spectacular
concentrations of natural stone
arches stands in the canyon country
of southern Utah. These impressive,
sweeping structures are the creations
of water and wind erosion.
Landscape Arch (above), the longest
natural stone span in the world,
reaches an awesome 291 feet.
Graceful Delicate Arch (left) is
another of the scores of dramatic
formations in Arches National
Park. Most massive of all
known spans, Rainbow Bridge
(right) arches 309 feet above a gorge.
Easily accessible from Lake Powell,
it is so close to water that one day
the reservoir may reach the base
of its natural piers and possibly
undermine it.

"Jewel of the Colorado"

Convoluted Lake Powell, slowly rising behind Glen Canyon Dam since 1964, twists its tortuous way through once-inaccessible canyons, now easily navigable by boat. River parties can enjoy the mirrored stillness of the lake (above) or disembark and explore side channels, such as the awesome Cathedral in the Desert (right), as yet unflooded. Hikers may surprise a sleepy young hawk or chance upon a cluster of butterfly weed.

Power and Power Boats

*Immense Glen Canyon Dam, rising 710 feet above the ancient bed of
the Colorado River, backs up Lake Powell which stretches 186 miles into
the red rock country. The lake's shoreline snakes in and out of more
than a hundred side canyons, rounds abrupt bends, and sweeps into bays
under overhanging rocks that loom overhead like giant band shells.
A challenging paradise for power boaters, the lake lures desert sailors to
explore the steep-walled side canyons, some so narrow that boats have
to be pushed through by hand, the crew lining the rails on both sides to
personally nudge the craft along.*

Canyonlands' Lunar Landscape

Much of it impenetrable, Canyonlands National Park is best explored from the air or from the bouncing seat of a four-wheel-drive vehicle. From above, the wildland takes on a bizarre beauty. Dramatic Chesler Park reveals itself as a doughnut-shaped basin, crossed by prospectors' jeep trails and rimmed by volcanic ridges. Ground-level travel is also memorable— but for different reasons. The drive starts on paved roads, switches to dirt, then to wheel tracks, then to no road at all. Passengers make it safely, but some have been known to get out and walk over parts of the dizzying route, such as the nose-dive below.

River of Adventure

From the air the spectacular confluence of the Green and Colorado rivers (right) is an unforgettable sight. The Green, threading in from the right, joins the Colorado just before it plunges into Cataract Canyon, a tumultuous passage through a 2,000-foot-deep trench in the sandstone. Boating down the rivers that twist through the eroded desert is a memorable blend of effortless drifting between mile-high cliffs and sandstone, with hardly a splash of water to dampen a sweatshirt, to moments of chaos and terror when the bulbous crafts wallow and thrash through boulder-choked rapids.

Majestic Monument Valley

Rising up from the floor of an immense bowl is a procession of reefs, buttes, and pinnacles—the last holdouts in a millennial drama of erosion. Formed of volcanic schists tougher than the earth's crust, these monoliths are still standing long after the surrounding terrain has been eaten away by eons of water, wind, and frost.

Sandblasted Landscape

Ribbed rock formations and powdery dunes scattered throughout the painted desert area testify to the shaping power of wind-driven sand. Centuries of scouring by abrasive gusts have carved the sandstone formations of an ancient lake bed into rounded forms that resemble solidified dunes (above). Powerful winds propel the living dunes in Monument Valley (right), barely held in check by tenacious plant materials, until they reach insurmountable barriers. Within the shifting dunes, pale lizards (left) and albino mice, color-adapted to the sands, live out their busy lives.

Spectacular Grazing Lands

*Slanting rays of the late afternoon sun highlight the sculptured
mesas and buttes of Monument Valley, an arid homeland to the nomadic
Navajo Indians, who graze their flocks on its sparse foliage.*

Home of the Wandering Navajos

Between 1000 and 1500, ancestors of the Navajos migrated to the Southwest from land farther north, perhaps the land that is now Canada. Today, the Navajo Indian Reservation covers northeastern Arizona and stretches briefly into southeastern Utah and northwestern New Mexico. Tribal headquarters for the Navajos is Window Rock, named after the weather-carved rock formation (right). Although many are abandoning traditional ways, some continue to carry on ancient customs and rites. Rugs are still woven in the open air here at Monument Valley, bread is fried on an open-air stove heated by stones, and, on ceremonial occasions, exquisite sand paintings are made with colored chips dribbled from a cupped hand.

First Desert City-Dwellers

In the heart of the painted desert live the Hopis, direct descendants of the ancient Anasazi city-builders, who reached their cultural peak in the 13th century at such sites as Betatakin (left), leaving scores of village ruins in the Southwest. Unlike the Navajos, the Hopis live almost entirely in villages. One of their settlements, Oraibi, is thought to have been occupied since about 1150. A more recent settlement is Walpi (above), established in this location around 1680. The Hopis rejected the early Spanish missionaries, keeping their culture free of Spanish-Christian influences. The most picturesque of their ancient customs are the snake dance, conducted with live rattlers, and the Kachina dances, in which masked participants accept petitions for rain, health, and good fortune. Another impressive ceremony finds Hopi maidens in elaborate butterfly costumes (right), ready to perform their dance.

Impregnable Canyon de Chelly

For about 2,000 years, spectacular Canyon de Chelly has been the home and refuge of desert dwellers. The first settlers were Basketmakers (approximately 1200 B.C.), followed by successive waves of canyon dwellers. The Anasazi people, ancestors of the Hopis, built houses in open caves along the canyon walls and beneath overhanging ledges on the canyon floor (1100-1300 A.D.). They were followed in the 1600s by the Navajos, new arrivals in the area. For three centuries the canyon's fortress-like walls, rising to heights of more than a thousand feet, provided sanctuary for the marauding Navajos. Spanish soldiers attempted without success to dislodge the Indians; later, the U.S. Cavalry tried for 20 years to drive them from the maze, finally starving them out in 1863 by destroying crops, orchards, and stock. The tribe was permitted to return to their ancestral homeland later and has occupied Canyon de Chelly since. Although it may seem deserted, the canyon is still quietly alive with Navajos who prefer the old ways.

Pictograph on canyon wall depicts Spanish soldiers and black-robed priest astride horses, a fearsome novelty to the Indians.

Bones of Dead Volcanoes

Many of the most striking rock formations in the Four Corners area are the remains of extinct volcanoes. These volcanoes originally consisted of a hard core covered by softer rock, lava, and ash. In time the softer parts eroded away, leaving the core to stand alone, a stark pinnacle rising from the sand. A one-time volcano, Shiprock, looming behind a battery of oil-pumping windmills, rises 1,400 feet above the desert in northwestern New Mexico. Another volcanic remain is Fisher Towers (right), forming a line of jagged pinnacles near Moab, Utah. Because of its gigantic size, the dominant peak is known as The Titan. In this dry desert setting, only a few plants survive, such as the yucca (left).

Early High-Rise

*For 100 years the famous Cliff
Palace at Mesa Verde swarmed with
people clambering up and down
rickety ladders to reach their
tiny apartments, some of which were
eight levels above the base. In
its heyday in the 13th century,
the palace was occupied by 200
residents, who tended crops in
the river bottoms and retreated to
their fortress home to ward off
enemy attacks. The palace
represented the climax of twelve
centuries of occupation of the Mesa
Verde area by the Anasazi, prehistoric
Indian tribes. The first masonry
pueblos were built on the mesas
beginning in 750 A.D. and a
flourishing culture developed over
the next two hundred years.
Beginning in 1200 the Anasazi
began to abandon their mesa top in
favor of more sheltered locations in
the enormous niches of Mesa Verde's
ramparts, probably for security
from enemy raids. By 1300 the
entire region was abandoned. The
remarkable ruins are protected
today by the National Park Service.
In some of the rooms, period pots
are on display.*

Lifeless Metropolis

The stillness of the deserted ruins of Chaco Canyon National Monument belies their history as one of the most important centers of commerce and culture in the prehistoric Southwest. A highly developed agricultural civilization reached its peak here in the 11th and 12th centuries. Most imposing of the structures within the monument is Pueblo Bonito, a complex that covered over three acres of ground, contained 800 rooms, and may have housed 1,200 inhabitants at the peak of its development. Construction began as early as 807 A.D. and continued for more than 300 years before the dwellings were abandoned early in the 12th century.

Chaco Canyon builders were expert masons. Wall sections remain in which the stones are so carefully fitted together that a knife blade can scarcely be inserted between them.

Three Centuries of Graffiti

The craggy mass of El Morro—Spanish for "bluff" or "headland"—looms above a herd of livestock in northwestern New Mexico. Preserved as a national monument, the towering sandstone bluff has served as both a landmark and a journal for early Southwest travelers. Indian hunters, Spanish conquistadors, and wagon train pioneers found shelter beneath its steep cliffs, quenched their thirst at the deep pool at the base of the cliffs (far right), and carved their names in the soft sandstone rock. Ramon Garcia Jurado scratched the elaborate inscription (right) in the cliffs in 1709 on his way to Zuni. Long before the Spaniards stopped here, prehistoric Indians had occupied and abandoned a pueblo atop the 200-foot-high rock.

Fossilized Wood Pile

Early Indians in the area pecked designs on large rocks, this one just outside Petrified Forest National Park. No one knows the meaning of the figures, which have withstood centuries of exposure to weather and vandals (note graffiti).

Log rounds, scattered in disarray down a desert hillside, look freshly cut—but they are actually solid rock, 200 millions years old. The mineralized logs started out as living trees in a prehistoric forest. When they died and fell, the trees were covered with sand, mud, and volcanic ash before they could decay. Then the wood was replaced cell by cell by silica in water filtering down through overlaying strata. Geologic upheaval eventually lifted the land, and wind and rain wore away the overlying sediments, exposing the trees. In the 1600s Indians stacked blocks of the petrified wood to form a large building, Agate House (above), still partly standing. This concentration of fossilized trees is protected in Petrified Forest National Park.

Heart of New Mexico

Cultural crossroad of the Southwest,

high in an enchanted land . . .

pueblo country . . . home to the artist

What is the mystique of New Mexico, the spell that justifies the official slogan "Land of Enchantment?"

Undeniably, part of the enthrallment is the gentle open landscape, rimmed with mountains, flooded in sunlight, and domed over with an intense blue. The clear air, still largely smogless, has a rain-washed freshness and is scented in the cool of the evening with the aroma of burning piñon logs rising from thousands of chimneys. Fall is particularly enchanting when the cottonwoods, aspens, and maples swath the Sangre de Cristo and Jemez mountains in gold, amber, and red, and clusters of red peppers hang drying in the sun.

But there is more to this region than scenic beauty. Picturesque little adobe villages, blending in with the earth from which they were fashioned, straggle along the winding roads. Pueblos dating back to prehistory are scattered over the river valleys. Each pueblo has its own honeycomb of apartments and its church and ceremonial kiva, the latter two representing a tolerant compromise between ancestral beliefs and the principles of Christianity introduced by the Spaniards four centuries ago. Even the cities have their ancient core—a Mexican plaza, squared off with stores and centered with the traditional bandstand.

Here is the meeting ground for three very different cultures: Indian, Latin, and Anglo. Descendants of the original Indian settlers live in the pueblos, and descendants of the quasi-conquerors of the 17th century, the Spanish-Mexicans, reside in small villages, strung out along the country roads. The Anglo latecomers, who have been on the scene a mere century and a half, live mostly in the big cities. This triangular

relationship produces a rich cultural mixture that is manifested in pageantry, handicrafts, cuisine, and methods of worship.

Links with the past have remained strong. Santa Fe, the oldest capital in the nation, proudly preserves relics that predate the Pilgrims by a decade or more, such as the Palace of the Governors (1610) which was headquarters of northern New Spain, and the oldest house (1200) and oldest church (1609) in the country. Ancient adobe houses sit haphazardly along streets that follow stream beds, and in the center of the city, the Plaza still provides a track for promenading—when it is not packed with tourists. The shady square was once the bustling terminus of the Santa Fe Trail, the main trade route to the Southwest from 1821 to the 1880s.

Taos, founded in 1615, was the setting for Indian raids and uprisings in the 18th century, a home for trappers and miners in the 1830s, and since the 1890s a haven for artists, writers, and musicians. This mountainous city retains much of its timeless appeal, even under the onslaught of tourists drawn to the art galleries, boutiques, craft shops, and ski slopes. Mushrooming Albuquerque, though it has expanded five-fold since 1950, carefully preserves its Old Town dating from 1700.

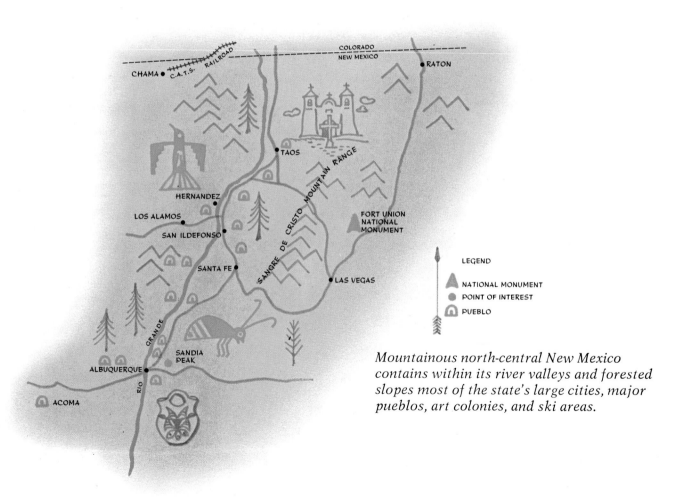

Mountainous north-central New Mexico contains within its river valleys and forested slopes most of the state's large cities, major pueblos, art colonies, and ski areas.

Drums throb and singers chant as costumed participants weave through
the ritualized movements of a Comanche dance at San Ildefonso Pueblo.
This January feast day is the pueblo's most important annual festival.

149

Winter Frosting in Taos

Winter snows bring a Christmas card look to Taos. Work animals in their shaggy winter coats are corraled close to the stables, the chapel at Ranchos de Taos wears an air of holiday tranquility, and roadside sculptures don white caps. At 7,000 feet Taos is no stranger to snow. In fact, snowfall is the principal source of precipitation in this land of little rain.

Craftsmen's Cornucopia

Santa Fe's founders introduced craft-making that is still practiced here. On display in shops is a tantalizing abundance of locally made woolens, candles, jewelry, necklaces, ceramic pieces, leather goods, and wrought iron whimseys. Famous open-air mart, the arcade of the Palace of the Governors (1610) sparkles with displays of jewelry, beads, and fabrics made by Indian craftsmen.

Santa Fe's Legendary Churches

Architectural interloper in a Spanish town, the serene façade of St. Francis Cathedral faces the Plaza area. The fifth church to occupy this site since 1610, it was built in 1869-84 by French missionary Archbishop Lamy. Thinly disguised under the name Archbishop Latour, Lamy has been immortalized in Willa Cather's Southwest classic, Death Comes for the Archbishop. *The cathedral's restrained style, derived from the Romanesque churches of Lamy's native province, contrasts sharply with the simple pueblo-style architecture of the Spanish missions. Nearby, a charming little Gothic chapel built by the Sisters of Loretto houses the "Miraculous Staircase," an elegantly formed spiral that was fashioned by a mysterious carpenter, the object of several enchanting legends.*

Skiing "Better than Switzerland"

From Thanksgiving to Easter, skiers flock to a half-dozen snow bowls conveniently close to Albuquerque, Taos, and Santa Fe. Rising through the clouds (above), a tram from Albuquerque ascends to Sandia Peak ski area, a scant five miles by cable from the downtown area. Nineteen miles from Taos (right), advanced skiers ride the chair lift to the top of heart-stopping Al's Run, described as "more like an elevator shaft than a ski run."

Moonrise over Hernandez

*The quick and the dead sleep peacefully together under a full moon
rising over Hernandez, a village dating back to the 17th century.*

The Magic Season

Cold weather lavishly transforms the look of the high mountains of New Mexico. The forest cover of aspen and conifers changes from all green to a bright gold-green tweed that blankets hundreds of square miles of the Sangre de Cristo Range. Along the watercourses of the upper Rio Grande near Santa Fe, the cottonwoods turn to dazzling gold. After the leaves fall, the white trunks of the bare aspen punctuate the lowering winter skies.

Hallmarks of Pueblo Architecture

Throughout New Mexico, pueblo-style buildings dominate the architectural scene. Evolved from the pueblos of centuries ago, this simple style is exquisitely adapted to a dry, timberless land where the only abundant building material is dirt. Hallmarks of the classic pueblo style are: thick walls formed of adobe block and structures seldom rising above one story without massive external support. To protect soluble adobe from the weather, exterior surfaces are plastered, all exposed edges are smoothly rounded, and gutter spouts are shaped to direct the runoff well beyond the wall line. Flat roofs are supported by log beams that project through the wall.

Fort near the Crossroad

The ruins of Fort Union, standing like soldiers at parade rest, spread out over 100 acres near the intersection of two arms of the once-populous Santa Fe Trail. The old wagon ruts can still be seen, most clearly from the air, cutting a wayward path through the prairie sod. Established in 1851 to protect wagon trains from bandits and Indian raiders, the fort was enlarged in 1863 to serve as a Union bastion in the Civil War. In the 1870s it was a staging area for horse soldiers who fought in the Indian wars that raged for 20 years. Deactivated in 1891, Fort Union's adobe buildings are slowly disintegrating.

Drawing by Frederic Remington accurately portrays the typical horse soldier of the frontier decades.

Land of Contrast

Barren desert and trout-filled lakes are only a few miles apart in the valley of the Rio Grande near Taos. The abrasive, silt-laden river has carved a deep gorge into a landscape so desolate that it was chosen as a site for astronauts to practice with an earth-bound version of the moon buggy prior to the 1971 lunar landing. Not far away from the simulated moonscape are scores of little lakes, such as this pine-rimmed tarn below.

Venerable Village Chapels

In the heart of every Spanish village stands a thick-walled adobe chapel, built in pueblo style and ornamented with simple designs. At Chimayo, below, the Sanctuario (1816) is famous for the curative powers attributed to the sacred sands beneath the floor. Hundreds of infirm believers journey to the "Lourdes of New Mexico," many leaving behind crutches, braces, and other devices upon which they had once depended.

Las Trampas (above), originally constructed in 1751 and rebuilt in 1969, is located on the high road to Taos. Boy guides like to tell tourists about mysterious rites conducted here by the Penitentes, a secretive group that is said to re-enact the Crucifixion with one of the members lashed to a cross for several painful hours. Oldest church in the United States, the San Miguel Chapel (left) in Santa Fe has been in use since the 17th century.

The Enduring Pueblos

Atop a 400-foot-high mesa west of Albuquerque is the pueblo of Acoma (right). Acknowledged to be the oldest continuously occupied town in the United States, the Sky City has probably been inhabited for at least a thousand years. Acoma is just one of a score of pueblos scattered over an arc stretching northeast from Zuni to Taos. Within these closely-knit, self-governing communities, life revolves around strong familial relationships, laced together with ancient ceremony and traditions.

The kiva (above at San Ildefonso), usually circular in form, is the heart of the religious life of the community that predates the introduction of Christianity by Spaniards four centuries ago. Many Pueblo celebrations blend both Christian and naturalistic rites, but the ceremonies held within the kiva are secret and sacred. Only ritual participants are permitted to enter the kiva, forbidden ground to others.

The Cities that Died of Fear

Immaculately fitted stonework is all that remains of "The Cities that Died of Fear," located southeast of Albuquerque. Founded by Spanish missionaries in the late 1620s, three immense missions were built by the Indians to serve a group of pueblos near present-day Mountainair. All were abandoned in the 1670s because of fierce raids by the Apaches. The Pueblo Indians took sanctuary with the colonies along the Rio Grande and never returned. The 200-year-old walls of the mother church still stand (left) at Abo State Monument. An unusual feature of this church was the inclusion of a kiva within the structure, representing a rare marriage of pagan and Christian faiths.

The extensive ruins at Gran Quivira National Monument (above) include the walls of the abandoned pueblo. Of this site a traveler of the 1890s commented: "On the Rhine it would be superlative; in the wilderness, it is a miracle."

Hoofing down the Highway

Traces of the Old West still survive in northern New Mexico, where motorists are accustomed to giving the right of way to flocks of sheep or herds of cattle that sometimes preempt highways on their way to market. In one of the longest cattle drives in the West, a herd of 600 Charolaise yearlings (right) plods 192 miles north into Colorado, accompanied by veteran and amateur cowpokes on the annual two week excursion. In winter the roads to Taos (below) are often clogged with bands of inconsiderate sheep, baaing their way to warmer pastures.

Steam Train to Yesterday

Weeds grow between the rails of the Cumbres & Toltec Scenic Railroad and the boxcars are remodeled, but the grandeur of the scenery, such as the Toltec Gorge (far right), coupled with good old steamy nostalgia keep the excursion trains of this old line filled to capacity. Built in 1880 the railroad operated until 1966. In 1970 it was saved from the scrap heap by an army of rail fans who contributed labor and money to its continuation. The track zigzags 64 crooked miles—almost all above the 8,000-foot mark— between Chama, New Mexico, and Antonito, Colorado.

Luminarias garland roof line, driveway, and garden paths of a Santa Fe home. At Ranchos de Taos, candles flicker on every accessible ledge on the chapel.

The Little Fires of Christmas

*Christmas comes to the Southwest in a blaze of twinkling lights.
Following an ancient Spanish tradition, tiny bonfires are set on Christmas
Eve in thousands of gardens and parks (above at Albuquerque's Old
Town Plaza), on walls, fences, and roof lines. The paraphernalia is simple:
the luminaria (or ferrolito to Texans) is made of a candle, inserted in an
open paper sack weighted with sand. The lights are set in place, often
at great risk of life and limb. At sundown on Christmas Eve, the wicks are
lighted; the gentle flames glow for several hours before burning out.*

179

Down the Rio Grande

Connecting link between two nations . . .

along the way: croplands, desert,

snowy peaks . . . path of the conquistadores

Considered solely as a watercourse, the Rio Grande is something of a disappointment. Except for its length—the second longest river in the nation—it has few memorable features. Generally unwadeable, uncrossable, unnavigable, and barely voluminous enough to supply the water needs of the communities and croplands along its length, the Rio Grande seems the most unaccommodating of rivers.

The off-and-on river runs full stream only part of the year, when it is swollen by snow melt or flash floods. The rest of the time it is either dried up completely in some stretches or slowed down to a shallow, brackish flow in others. It can only be navigated in small boats for short distances, and then only downstream. It is a difficult river to cross. In the northern section of New Mexico, the Rio Grande courses down a deep gorge, so steep-walled that it cannot be traversed except by high-level bridges. Even after the river reaches the broad valley below the gorge, it is treacherous to ford because of quicksands that mire horses, cattle, and swimmers. Dams have tamed its once rampaging floods but have almost drained the river dry to supply farms and cities along the way.

Yet grudging as the Rio Grande seems to be, it has long been a life-giving source to the peoples of New Mexico and has helped determine the course of the state's history. A favored location for settlements, most of the pueblos were established near its banks. Spanish explorers trudged northward along the river in search of the fabled cities of gold in the 1540s, and a half-century later, colonists founded outposts at Santa Fe and Taos. When they were driven out in 1680 by a revolt of the Pueblo Indians, the Spaniards retreated in disarray down the river valley.

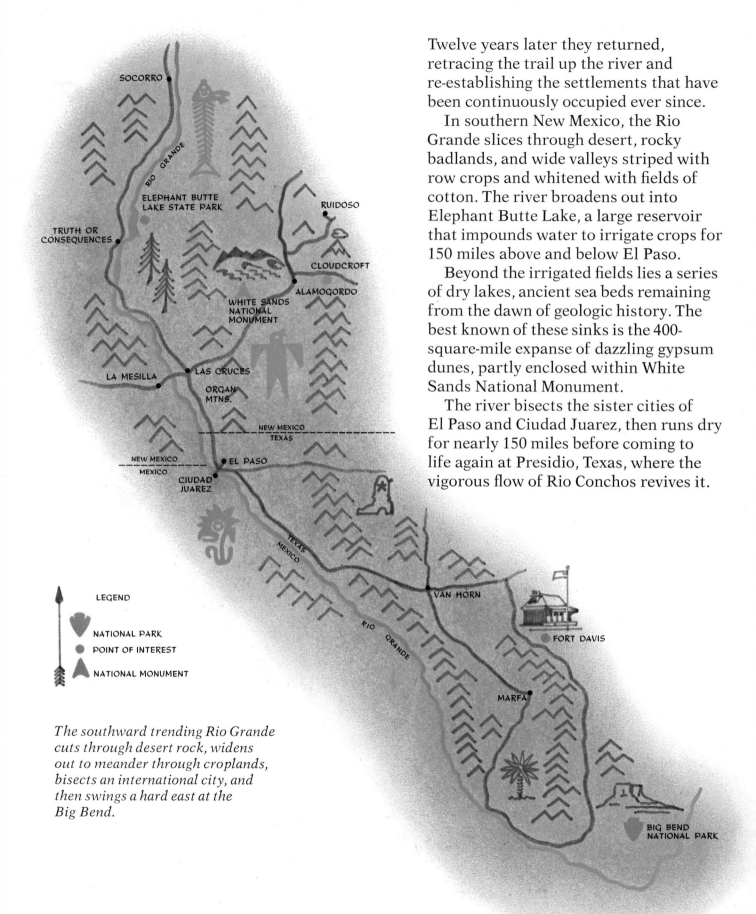

Twelve years later they returned, retracing the trail up the river and re-establishing the settlements that have been continuously occupied ever since.

In southern New Mexico, the Rio Grande slices through desert, rocky badlands, and wide valleys striped with row crops and whitened with fields of cotton. The river broadens out into Elephant Butte Lake, a large reservoir that impounds water to irrigate crops for 150 miles above and below El Paso.

Beyond the irrigated fields lies a series of dry lakes, ancient sea beds remaining from the dawn of geologic history. The best known of these sinks is the 400-square-mile expanse of dazzling gypsum dunes, partly enclosed within White Sands National Monument.

The river bisects the sister cities of El Paso and Ciudad Juarez, then runs dry for nearly 150 miles before coming to life again at Presidio, Texas, where the vigorous flow of Rio Conchos revives it.

The southward trending Rio Grande cuts through desert rock, widens out to meander through croplands, bisects an international city, and then swings a hard east at the Big Bend.

River runners find the tributaries of the Rio Grande a challenge to their skills. However, narrow, twisting, and almost inaccessible Mariscal Canyon is safe for canoers because of its lack of turbulence.

183

A Fire-Scarred Land

Violent geomorphic upheavals have left scars on the land through which the Rio Grande passes. To the east of the river, the sawtoothed profile of the Organ Mountains (above), named for a fancied resemblance to an enormous pipe organ, edges the horizon. A volcanic dike, the fire-born range has stood for eons while the surrounding land has eroded away. To the west of the river, blackened lava beds (right) remain from an eruption 10,000 years ago. A reminder of a more recent upheaval is a stark monument (left), that marks the site of the first atomic bomb explosion, July 16, 1945.

White Mirror to the Sky

So pure is the dazzling white of the gypsum dunes at White Sands National Monument (below) that the granules reflect the coloring of the sky. The mimicking dunes wear a bluish tint under a clear sky, turn gray under a lowering storm, or reflect the rosy hues of sunrise and sunset. Ceaselessly on the move, the dunes often leave behind plants, such as the yucca (right), with their roots mercilessly exposed.

Hooded against wind and sun, colorful picnic units that resemble desert sailboats are mounted on skids so they can be shifted to keep up with the wandering dunes.

Recreational Highlands

*Topped by 12,003-foot Sierra Blanca (above), the mountains
in southern New Mexico tower above the level plains, only a few miles
east of barren White Sands. A forested refuge from the heat in summer
and a crowded sports area in winter, the range is a recreational beehive.
This profusion of resorts, cabin towns, campgrounds, picnic sites, trout
streams, and lakes is interspersed among the rangelands of the Mescalero
Indians and draws vacationers from the surrounding plains. Many come
to place bets at "America's richest horse race" at Ruidoso Downs; golfers
head for Cloudcroft, where at 9,000 feet golf balls fly for added distance.
The Sierra Blanca ski area (right), operated by the Mescaleros, accounts
for more ticket sales than any other ski bowl in the state—probably
because it is the ski area closest to the major cities of West Texas.*

Guardians of the Frontier

Bugle calls have long been stilled at scores of abandoned army posts scattered throughout the Southwest. The tin-roofed officers' quarters baking in the sun at Fort Davis (left), constructed in 1854, have not echoed to an assembly call since 1891.

Restored adobe barracks (above), a topiary horse, and an old cavalry recruiting poster enliven Old Fort Bliss (1848), now a military museum in El Paso.

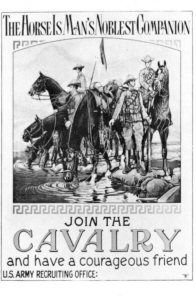

Twin Cities on the Pass

Located strategically on the lowest pass through the tip of the Rockies, the twin cities of El Paso and Ciudad Juarez grew up as trade centers. Looking from the hills behind El Paso toward the Mexican hillside, the two cities appear as one (right), the burgeoning business district of El Paso blending with the Mexican metropolis across the river. The citizens of the two cities share strong commercial and familial ties—some 65 per cent of the surnames in El Paso are Latin in origin. One of the world's few international streetcars (left) rattles back and forth, night and day, between the two cities.

The mighty Rio Grande dwindles to a quiet, shallow stream by the time it reaches El Paso and flows under the International Bridge (boundary designation is on lower part of middle support).

Ciudad Juarez

An engrossing city, Ciudad Juarez is a potpouri of opposites — antiquity and ultramodernity, poverty and luxury, honest and dubious business dealings. A pigeon stops to rest on the face of the 18th-century cathedral clock (above) that boldly tolls the hour. The sumptuous modern Art Museum (left) houses an excellent collection of colonial paintings. In the courtyard, artists earn a modest living painting to order. Shops range from those rarely seen by tourists (such as the farmers' market at right, where a hard bargain can be sealed if you know the rules) to elaborately set tourist traps shown below (packed to the rafters with kitsch, but salted with a sprinkling of truly valuable objects).

Homage to Our Lady of Guadalupe

As in every Mexican community on the sacred dawn of December 12th, the faithful of Juarez gather to venerate the Virgin of Guadalupe, Patroness of all the Americas. The religious feast surpasses all other sacred days in the fervor of its celebration. Crowds mass before the cathedral to watch the procession carrying holy relics. Brilliantly costumed dancers perform in the square, and the traditional bullfight ends the festival.

The ceremonies start at midnight in the Cathedral of Our Lady of Guadalupe, rising next to a chapel on the site of the original mission (1659). From dawn to dusk, crowds accompanied by singing mariachis heap flowers upon the altar.

Badlands of the Big Bend

The Rio Grande lives up to its boastful name in Big Bend National Park (right), where it slices through three mountain ranges, leaving behind gorges such as the precipitous Santa Elena Canyon (1,500 feet) on the right. Much of the land through which the river flows is semiarid, high desert, tufted with cactus and forested with ocotillo. Above these rolling badlands tower the arid Chisos Mountains, cresting at 8,000 feet. Historically, this wilderness has been regarded as either a dreaded obstacle to travelers or a welcome refuge for renegades. Apache chiefs directed their thunderous bands from strongholds in these mountains for forty years before they were finally subdued in 1886. Their old hideaways are now park tourist attractions.

The park harbors an abundance of wildlife. The ringtail cat, cousin of the raccoon, favors cliffs and rocky canyons. Gambel's quail are seen in Big Bend's drier areas. And debonair javelinas, traveling in groups, are often encountered in the lowlands.

By the Bend of the River

Visitors to the lowlands of Big Bend National Park can freely wander back and forth between the United States and Mexico by crossing the shallow Rio Grande at Boquillas. Those who cross into Mexico cannot penetrate very far to the south; passage is blocked by a vast waterless, untracked, and sparsely settled area that stretches for hundreds of miles. Boquillas itself is so isolated that Mexican border patrolmen receive their salaries by mail in the United States.

Occasionally seen in Big Bend's thicketed areas and remote canyons, ocelots have migrated here from Latin American jungles. Though not a true desert dweller, this graceful cat has successfully adapted to desert living conditions.

The High Plains

Land of the big sky and invisible horizon . . .

of oceans of wheat, large ranches,

nodding oil pumps . . . last stand of the cowboy

The High Plains of west Texas and eastern New Mexico are a land of solitude and loneliness, of humming telephone wires and blowing tumbleweeds, a place where the sky melts imperceptibly into the horizon.

This region, also known as the *Llano Estacado* or "Staked Plains" (a term of unknown meaning), is a dry, treeless extension of the Great Plains of the Midwest. Oceanlike in its limitless expanse, it provides an unimpeded playground for the winds, which blow ceaselessly, sometimes softly and indolently, sometimes with great violence.

Originally carpeted with grass, the plains area was once the home range of buffalo, antelope, multitudes of prairie dogs and jack rabbits and their predators, the coyote and plains wolf. The plentiful supply of game animals made the region a vast larder for the plains Indians who hunted here.

White men converted the hunting preserve into a cattle range. In time, thousands of longhorns, jollied along by swarms of cowboys, grazed a path to market. Wherever vaqueros made camp or trains stopped to load the bellowing cattle, small settlements formed that later grew into cities. Some were appropriately named: Lariat, Muleshoe, Hereford, Bovina, Matador, Bronco, Rodeo, Spur. Although the heyday of the cowhand is now past, cowboy reunions still attract throngs of grizzled veterans of the range, and rodeos, both scheduled and impromptu, take place throughout the area.

When farmers settled in this treeless, waterless region, they planted their own trees, often specimens nostalgically imported from back home, and they harnessed the wind to draw water from deep wells. As they established themselves on the land, they encountered stubborn opposition from stockmen who resisted this encroachment on their historic open range. Beginning in the 1870s, farmers fenced their acreages with the revolutionary new invention barbed wire, labeled the "devil's hatband." Economical, practical, and efficient, this barrier forever sealed off the open path to cattle markets and changed the plains economy. Now, immense ranches of wheat, maize, sorghum, alfalfa, and

cotton cover hundreds of square miles. Deep beneath these fertile farmlands lies one of the nation's largest preserves of natural gas and petroleum, brought to the surface by donkey-headed oil pumps.

Besides fighting off cattlemen, the farmers waged a relentless war against the inexhaustible population of prairie dogs and jack rabbits that consumed their crops. The prairie dogs were eventually eliminated; today the only signs of this plump ground squirrel are a few colonies in open-air museums and a place name in Texas: the Prairie Dog Town Fork of the Red River. The unconquerable jack rabbit, finally reduced to manageable numbers, is similarly honored in retrospect. In Odessa, Texas, stands a 10-foot statue, "The World's Largest Jack Rabbit," bearing a plaque with an historical summary on one side and a recipe for rabbit stew on the other.

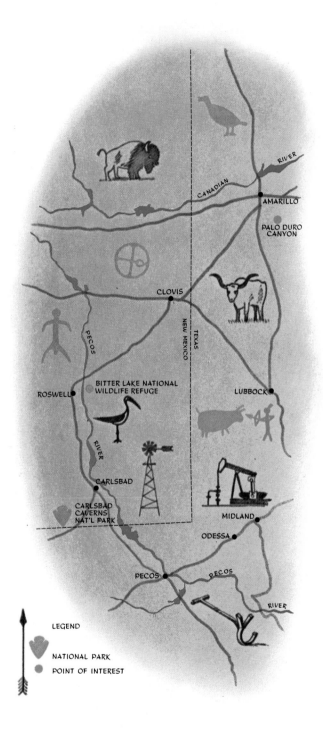

LEGEND

NATIONAL PARK
POINT OF INTEREST

The High Plains, an arm of the Great Plains, sweeps from the Caprock (a natural barrier running down the Texas Panhandle) deep into New Mexico.

Donkey-headed oil pumps nod tirelessly in the midst of endless croplands throughout the High Plains. Underground lies one of the nation's richest oil reserves; topside is one of the most productive farming areas in the Southwest.

Wild Lands, Wild Animals

Remnants of a once-wild land still exist in the
Panhandle. Palo Duro Canyon (right) slices
a deep trough through the level farmlands,
carving the earth into buttes, spires, and eroded
cliffs. Animal survivors from once-numerous
species live protected lives within game
preserves. A few hundred antelope near Palo
Duro Canyon are all that remain from the
millions that used to roam the plains. The
prairie dog foursome (left) are members of a
protected colony at Amarillo. At one time
the most prevalent animal of the plains, these
oversized ground squirrels were the staple
diet of prairie predators.

Windmills and Waterholes

The tall, spindly figure of an occasional windmill, creaking and complaining in the wind, is often the only visible evidence of man's presence in the open plains. Without these lanky contrivances, the land would still be open prairie. The windmill brought water to a riverless land, opened it to farming, and created artificial waterholes for cattle. Now being displaced by electric pumps, the windmill is still the symbol of the conquest of the prairie.

Land of the Big Blow

Churning up patterns of menacing beauty, a storm drives across the Panhandle. Trees lean with the wind, windmills race, lightning forks down from the black sky, and cattle huddle behind billboards to escape the driving sleet. Like the open sea, the high plains are the playground of strong winds and dramatic storms that blow unimpeded across the flat surface.

At Sea in Wheat

Wheat farms as vast as small counties blanket the open plains. Highly mechanized, the farms are gang-harvested by giant combines that chomp their dusty way through the fields. Still, the rural look persists—roads untouched by the trim discipline of the county system slither an uncertain path up the furrowed slopes.

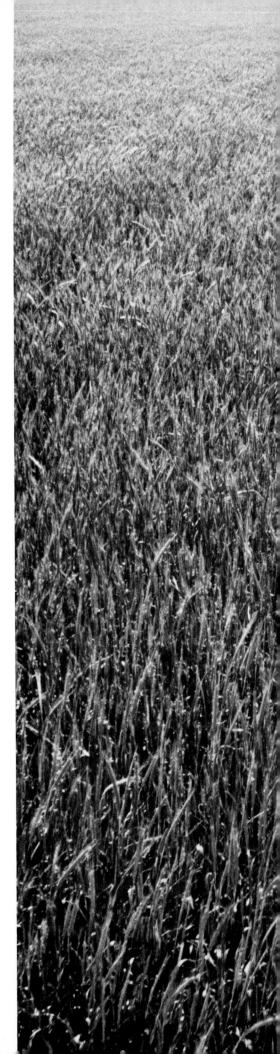

Land of the Longhorn

Cattle are raised on land too barren for cultivation. Livestock graze over the immense ranches, then are herded to feed lots for fattening. Rodeos, spontaneous and staged, erupt at every shipping point. Occasionally someone tries his luck at Brahma busting.

Ornery and tough, able to survive on little water and less grass, the Texas longhorn is being re-bred for a possible comeback on the more arid rangelands.

Cowboy Country

*On the great ranches of the Texas
and New Mexico plains, the cowboy
carries out his timeless tasks
with relaxed grace. A mule-drawn
wagon leisurely follows the hands
to the range camp, hauling firewood
to the fuelless site. On pasture
lands cowboys stir a herd of
longhorns into a frantic gallop
for the corral gate.*

In the early morning, a cowboy ropes his mount for the day from the remuda. On a Saturday night, a ranch hand unable to make it to town dispels his boredom with gravity-defying rope tricks.

Refuges for Boats and Birds

In an area with few running streams and fewer lakes, the ponds and reservoirs scattered over the flat land take on special importance. Waterfowl alight to rest—when the reeds are not occupied by hunters and decoys—and small craft criss-cross every body of water that is large enough to float a tub. On the larger reservoirs where long narrow lakes stretch miles up river valleys, extensive marina developments cater to landlocked sailors.

Technology on the High Plains

Helium-filled balloon at Roswell, New Mexico, takes off for the stratosphere, carrying instruments to probe weather secrets of this and other planets. Nearby, an immense self-propelled drilling rig wanders purposefully over the flat lands, pausing here and there to tap into the vast underground petroleum reserves. Found also at Roswell, the neat laboratories of Robert H. Goddard, the Wizard of Rocketry, are meticulously preserved as a museum to honor the work of this space age pioneer. These are some of the visible clues indicating that this region, lying above one of the nation's richest petroleum fields, is a leader in the technology of petroleum engineering and solid-fuel propellants.

A Nightmare Underground

A fantasy world of weird rock formations extends for miles under the desert at Carlsbad Caverns National Park. Only a small portion (about 23 miles) of this nether world has been explored, and only three of these miles have been opened to the public.

PHOTOGRAPHERS

ANSEL ADAMS: 158-159. **WILLIAM APLIN:** 14-15; 95; 111 bottom; 140; 142 bottom. **HANS BAERWALD:** 8; 24 bottom right. **LEN BOUCHE:** 152 bottom right. **BILL BRIDGES:** 36 bottom; 37 bottom; 60; 68; 69; 106 top; 107; 160 bottom; 171; 192 bottom; 193; 195. **RICHARD WEYMOUTH BROOKS:** 20 bottom right. **GUS BUNDY:** 66-67 top. **BUREAU OF LAND MANAGEMENT:** 57. **ROBERT CASPER:** 94 bottom; 156; 179; 189. **BILL CHENEY:** 152 bottom, second from left; 152 top right; 152 center. **CLYDE CHILDRESS:** 23 top. **GLENN CHRISTIANSEN:** 33 top; 34-35 top; 36-37 top; 39 top; 45; 94 top; 108-109; 128; 130 bottom; 132; 133 bottom; 152 center left; 152 bottom center; 153. **BOB CLEMENZ:** 124-125; 187. **BILL CLOUGH:** 209; 210; 211; 212. **KENYON COBEAN:** 213; 214; 215 top; 218; 219 bottom; 220; 221. **DOLLY CONNELLY:** 42 bottom; 43; 47; 74; 115. **BRAD COOPER:** 192 top; 196. **ED COOPER:** 4; 9; 13; 31; 48; 49; 50-51; 63; 70-71; 75; 78-79; 80; 81; 93; 97 top; 102; 103; 114; 118; 127; 131; 135; 136 bottom; 137; 144 bottom; 145; 184-185 top; 222; 223. **CARI CREWS:** 40. **RICHARD DAWSON:** 35 bottom. **CARLOS ELMER:** 88-89; 180-181. **PHYLLIS ELVING:** 170. **RICHARD FALLER:** 162; 163; 172; 173; 219 top. **WILLIAM FETTKETHER:** 56 top. **EDWARD C. FORSYTH:** 130 top. **GERALD R. FREDRICK:** 24 bottom left. **LAURA GILPIN:** 165; 166. **WAYNE GRAVNING:** 167 bottom; 168; 185 bottom. **FRED HANKINS:** 19; 53. **HARPER AND ROW:** 106 bottom. **C. W. HERBERT (WESTERN WAYS FEATURES):** 26-27 top. **CARROLL ANN HODGES:** 11. **PHILIP HYDE:** 62; 82; 83; 84; 85; 86; 87; 101 top; 116 bottom left; 117. **HAROLD L. JAMES:** 142 top; 143. **JEAN & TROX:** 100. **OLIVER JOHNSON:** 133 top. **PAUL C. JOHNSON:** 191. **RUTH KIRK:** 44 top; 44 bottom left. **RUTH AND LOUIS KIRK:** 23 bottom; 30; 44 bottom right; 126; 130 center; 198. **LAKE HAVASU CITY:** 58; 59. **WALTER LANDOR ASSOCIATES:** 26 bottom. **JOHN LARSEN:** 119. **BOB LEATHERMAN:** 56 bottom. **MARTIN LITTON:** 46; 101 bottom; 122. **LOS ALAMOS LABORATORY:** 184 bottom. **RAY MANLEY:** 42 top. **BUDDY MAYS:** 176 top; 188; 194; 197; 206 top; 208 bottom. **DANA C. MORGENSON:** 91; 160 top. **DAVID MUENCH:** 7; 22; 38; 61; 76; 98; 129; 139; 200. **JOSEF MUENCH:** 2; 16; 18; 20 top left; 20 top right; 27 bottom; 65; 111 top; 116 top; 144 top; 199; 207. **BRAD MUSICK:** 216; 217. **LEONARD NADEL:** 64. **NASA:** 99 bottom; 167 top. **NATIONAL PARK SERVICE:** 41. **ANNE NOGGLE:** 161. **DON NORMARK:** 32. **WILLIS PETERSON:** 25; 201. **PHOTOFIND (ROBERT AMES):** 73. **BLAIR PITTMAN:** 183. **ROBERT POTTS:** 20 bottom left; 20 bottom center; 20 left, second from bottom. **RUTH AND CHUCK POWELL:** 176 bottom; 177. **BETTY RANDALL:** 20 center top; 20 center, second from top; 20 center, second from bottom; 20 left, second from top; 116 bottom right; 186. **BILL REAVES:** 208 top. **SPENCER ROSS:** 152 bottom left; 152 right center; 152 center top. **JOHN RUNNING:** 134; 141; 149; 152 top left. **HOPE RYDEN:** 24 top; 67 bottom. **FREDERIC SHIDLER, M.D.:** 92; 96; 97 bottom. **JOHN STEBBINS:** 146-147; 151; 175; 178 bottom. **TEXAS HIGHWAY DEPARTMENT:** 202-203; 205; 206 bottom; 215 bottom. **TEXAS TOURIST DEVELOPMENT AGENCY:** 190. **TOM TRACY:** 33 bottom; 39 bottom. **U. S. GEOLOGICAL SURVEY (CENTER OF ASTROGEOLOGY):** 99 top. **DON VALENTINE:** 28-29; 77. **DARWIN VAN CAMPEN:** 21. **DARROW M. WATT:** 54; 55. **ROBERT WENKAM:** 102; 104; 105; 112; 120; 121; 123. **C. SCOTT WILSON:** 12; 138; 150 bottom; 154; 155; 169. **BARON WOLMAN:** 150 top; 157; 174. **JOHN V. YOUNG:** 136 top.

FRONT COVER: Chesler Park, in Canyonlands National Park; photograph by Richard Weymouth Brooks. (Note: the image is reversed for design reasons.) **BACK COVER:** Mission San Xavier del Bac, in Arizona; photograph by John Running.

ENDPAPER: Navajo yei rug from Shiprock region in New Mexico. From the private collection of *Sunset* Magazine.

This book was printed and bound by Kingsport Press, Kingsport, Tennessee, from litho film prepared by Balzer-Shopes Litho Plate Company, San Francisco, California. Body type is Aster composed by Paul O. Giesey/Adcrafters, Portland, Oregon. Type for heads is Windsor photocomposed by Timely Typography, San Francisco, California.